Hyrox Training Mastery:
Prepare, Perform, and Dominate

By: Alex Harper, MS & Taylor Reed
Edited & Published by: Creative Pages

Hyrox Training Mastery by Creative Pages Publisher

Welcome to Creative Pages!

Discover a World of Creativity and Inspiration

At Creative Pages, we're passionate about crafting journals and books that cater to a variety of needs and interests. Whether you're seeking a thoughtful journal to capture your ideas, a low-content planner to organize your days, or an immersive read to dive into, we have something for everyone.

What We Do:

- **Journals:** Designed to inspire and motivate, helping you capture your thoughts, dreams, and daily reflections.
- **Low-Content Books:** Perfect for those who need guided prompts, planners, and trackers to stay organized and productive.
- **High-Content Books:** Immersive reads that offer a deep and engaging experience.

Don't Miss Out!

Browse Our Full Range on Amazon & Try Our Other Books and Journals:
Discover new favorites and essential tools for your daily life and creative journey.

Join Our Community!

- **Follow Us on Instagram:** Stay updated on new releases, special offers, and behind-the-scenes content. Follow us at @creativepagespublisher and become part of our vibrant community!
- **Get in touch:** We'd love to hear from you! For any questions, feedback, or collaborations, email us at creativepagespublisher@gmail.com

OUTLINE

Introduction: Why Hyrox?

If you've been to a Hyrox event, you know one thing for sure: it's not your average race. The booming sound of energetic music, the unmistakable clang of weights, and the sight of athletes pushing themselves to their physical and mental limits—it's all part of an electrifying experience. But what exactly is Hyrox, and why is it quickly becoming one of the world's fastest-growing sports?

What is Hyrox, and Why is It Growing?

Hyrox is a **functional fitness race** that combines running with various workout stations, including sled pushes, rowing, burpees, and more. Unlike traditional races or obstacle course events, Hyrox is designed to test both endurance and strength in a format that is challenging yet accessible to all fitness levels. You don't need to be an elite athlete to participate; you just need the determination to push yourself through a series of high-intensity exercises while also covering a distance of 8 kilometers.

This combination of **functional fitness** and **endurance-based competition** taps into the global fitness trend of combining **strength and cardio**. Functional fitness has shown benefits in improving overall health and reducing injury risk compared to isolated exercises (McGill, 2016). Whether you're a CrossFit enthusiast, a triathlete or a long-distance runner, Hyrox offers a platform that caters to a wide variety of athletes. And that's where the sport's beauty lies—**anyone can do it**. From seasoned competitors to fitness newcomers, Hyrox is designed to push each participant to their personal limits, making it an addictive challenge.

The sport has seen rapid growth across Europe and North America, with events being held in major cities like Berlin, London, New York, and Chicago. The appeal of Hyrox lies in its **standardized format**—whether you're competing in Berlin or Boston, the course is always the same, so you can compare your time globally and track your improvements. Plus, the professional organization and exhilarating atmosphere at each event make it feel like you're part of something bigger. Hyrox isn't just a race—it's a global community of athletes.

A Brief History of Hyrox

Hyrox was co-founded in 2017 by **Christian Toetzke**, an innovator in the world of sports marketing, and **Moritz Fürste**, a former Olympic gold medalist in field hockey. Their vision was to create an event that merges endurance racing with functional fitness, filling a gap in the fitness competition market. It was launched in Germany and quickly gained traction, attracting athletes of all kinds (Toetzke & Fürste, 2019).

By 2019, the sport had spread internationally, gaining recognition in North America and beyond. Major sponsorships and partnerships with fitness brands further propelled Hyrox into the spotlight, and it continues to grow exponentially. The appeal lies not only in the race itself but also in the fact that competitors are encouraged to **set personal records** and track their progress. It's not just about winning—it's about continuously improving (Hyrox, 2021).

The Ideal Athlete Profile: Functional Fitness Meets Endurance

What sets Hyrox apart from other endurance or obstacle races is that it's not just about one thing. It doesn't matter if you're a world-class runner or can deadlift twice your bodyweight—Hyrox demands a **balanced athlete** who can handle both **strength and endurance**.

Hyrox tests your ability to **run fast and perform heavy functional exercises** back-to-back, without rest. For example, after running a kilometer, you're immediately thrown into a physically demanding task like pushing a sled loaded with weight. This is where functional fitness comes in. Functional fitness refers to exercises that mimic real-world activities, enhancing not just strength but also **mobility, flexibility, and coordination** (McGill, 2016).

In Hyrox, you need to be able to run efficiently, but you also need to recover quickly between workout stations. This requires a high level of cardiovascular fitness, muscular endurance, and mental fortitude. Studies have shown that integrating high-intensity interval training (HIIT) with functional fitness exercises improves overall fitness levels, particularly for combined strength and endurance demands (Laursen & Jenkins, 2002). A well-rounded Hyrox athlete must be able to **maintain a strong pace while performing physically taxing movements**, which is why training for Hyrox requires a unique blend of running, weightlifting, and HIIT.

Who is This Book For?

Whether you're preparing for your first Hyrox event or looking to dominate your next competition, this book is for you. We'll cover everything you need to know to improve your **strength, endurance, and overall performance**. From beginners who are just dipping their toes into the world of functional fitness to experienced athletes aiming for the podium, this guide has something for everyone.

This book will help you navigate:

- **Training Plans**: We'll break down a 12-week progressive plan tailored to your current fitness level.
- **Race Day Strategy**: Learn how to pace yourself through the event's unique combination of running and workouts.
- **Mindset**: Discover the mental tools to push through the hardest parts of the race.

- **Nutrition and Recovery**: Fuel your body for performance and recovery like a pro.

By the end of this book, you'll have everything you need to **prepare, perform, and dominate** your next Hyrox race. Whether your goal is to finish strong, improve your time, or take home the gold, this book will equip you with the tools and knowledge to reach your full potential.

Key Takeaways

- Hyrox is a functional fitness race that combines endurance and strength, making it appealing to athletes of all kinds.
- The sport has quickly gained popularity across Europe and North America due to its inclusive nature and standardized format.
- Hyrox athletes need a well-rounded balance of running, strength, and recovery to succeed.
- This book is for athletes at every level, offering training plans, race strategies, and mental toughness tips.

Chapter 1: Understanding the Hyrox Event

As mentioned in the introduction, Hyrox is a fitness race that's not just about speed or strength—it's about endurance, power, and grit. Whether you've done marathons, CrossFit, or Spartan Races, the unique format of Hyrox sets it apart. But before diving into how you can train for it, let's first break down what makes Hyrox so special and why it's growing in popularity worldwide.

The Hyrox Race Format: A Detailed Breakdown

At its core, Hyrox consists of a straightforward but grueling format: **eight kilometers of running, paired with eight functional workout stations**. Unlike obstacle course races (OCRs) like Spartan, Hyrox doesn't test your ability to climb walls or crawl under barbed wire. Instead, it's a controlled and standardized indoor event where every athlete, no matter where in the world, faces the same course.

Here's how it goes:

1. **1K Run**
2. **Ski Erg (1,000 meters)**
3. **1K Run**
4. **Sled Push (165-275 lbs depending on the division)**
5. **1K Run**
6. **Sled Pull (110-165 lbs)**
7. **1K Run**
8. **Burpee Broad Jumps (80 meters)**
9. **1K Run**
10. **Rowing (1,000 meters)**
11. **1K Run**
12. **Farmers Carry (32 kg per hand for men, 24 kg for women)**
13. **1K Run**
14. **Sandbag Lunges (30 meters with a 20 kg sandbag)**
15. **1K Run**
16. **Wall Balls (100 reps with a 20 lb ball for men and 14 lb for women)**

This combination of **running and high-intensity functional workouts** ensures that Hyrox tests both your cardiovascular and muscular endurance. It's not just about being able to run fast or lift heavy; it's about doing both in quick succession. This back-to-back structure adds a unique challenge, pushing participants to balance their energy and maintain high performance across a variety of movements.

The Power of Strength, Endurance, and Grit

What makes Hyrox particularly demanding is the **dynamic combination of strength and endurance**. It's rare to find an event that challenges both in such a balanced way. Athletes can't just rely on their running stamina or strength alone—they need to master both.

Strength is essential for exercises like the sled push/pull, farmers carry, and wall balls. These movements require raw power and muscular endurance, particularly in your **lower body and core**. Scientific research supports that exercises like these, which mimic functional, everyday movements, improve **total body fitness** and help prevent injury by developing real-world strength (Bishop et al., 2019).

Endurance is equally crucial. You may be able to crush a sled push, but can you quickly transition to a kilometer run afterward? The constant shifts between running and functional exercises keep your heart rate elevated, requiring a high level of cardiovascular fitness (Joyner & Coyle, 2008). Runners often struggle with heavy lifting, and lifters can find long-distance running a challenge, but Hyrox athletes have to blend the two efficiently.

But above all, **grit**—that mental toughness that keeps you going when your muscles are screaming and you're gasping for breath—might be the most important quality. Studies show that mental resilience is a key component in performance, particularly in endurance-based events (Duckworth & Quinn,

2009). Hyrox athletes push themselves not just physically but mentally, testing their ability to persist through discomfort and exhaustion.

What Makes Hyrox Unique?

There are plenty of fitness events out there—CrossFit, Spartan Races, Triathlons—but Hyrox carves out its niche by combining elements of both **strength sports and endurance racing** in a controlled, competitive environment. Let's compare these fitness races vs Hyrox.

- **Hyrox vs. CrossFit**

CrossFit is known for its varied, functional workouts, and in many ways, it shares common ground with Hyrox. Both require participants to be well-rounded athletes. However, CrossFit competitions often vary in format and exercises, with events focusing more on Olympic lifting, gymnastics, and high-skill movements like handstand walks or muscle-ups. Hyrox, on the other hand, sticks to its standardized format, which means you always know what to expect. This makes it more accessible to athletes who want consistency and predictability in their training (CrossFit Journal, 2021).

- **Hyrox vs. Spartan Race**

Spartan Races are more about overcoming physical obstacles in an outdoor setting, such as climbing walls or jumping over fire. While Spartan does challenge strength, it places a greater emphasis on agility and specific obstacle skills. Hyrox, by contrast, keeps the competition indoors and focused on functional movements that test brute strength and endurance. There are no surprises in Hyrox; it's you versus the course, which can be a welcome relief for athletes who prefer the certainty of gym-based exercises (Spartan Race, 2021).

- **Hyrox vs. Triathlon**

A triathlon combines three endurance sports—swimming, cycling, and running. While it shares Hyrox's focus on endurance, Hyrox goes a step further by incorporating strength and high-intensity functional exercises. Triathletes may excel at endurance, but they often lack the functional strength needed for exercises like sled pushing or burpee broad jumps. This makes Hyrox a different kind of challenge, offering a unique test of overall fitness (Jönsson, 2018).

Key Takeaways:

- Hyrox combines eight running intervals with eight functional fitness stations, testing both endurance and strength.
- Athletes need to excel at both cardiovascular fitness and strength-based exercises like sled pushes, farmers carries, and wall balls.
- What sets Hyrox apart from other fitness events is its blend of consistent, standardized challenges that

balance endurance and functional strength in an indoor setting.

- Unlike CrossFit or Spartan Races, Hyrox offers a predictable competition format that is ideal for athletes of all levels.

Chapter 2: Preparing Your Body for Hyrox

The nature of this sport demands versatility—blending running, functional strength, and high-intensity circuits into one continuous challenge. Whether you're an experienced athlete or new to the fitness world, preparing your body for Hyrox requires a focused approach to meet the event's diverse physical demands. This chapter will help you assess your current fitness, set realistic goals, and map out a plan to dominate on race day.

The Physical Demands of Hyrox

At first glance, Hyrox seems like a simple mix of running and workout stations, but it's far more complex. Each element demands a combination of **endurance, power, and high-intensity output**, and understanding these demands is key to successful training.

Running

Hyrox requires you to run a total of 8 kilometers, broken up into 1K intervals between functional workout stations. While running alone isn't overly challenging for most people, the **accumulated fatigue** from the strength and conditioning exercises between the runs means you need to develop solid cardiovascular endurance (Knechtle et al., 2020).

Functional Strength

Exercises like the sled push/pull, sandbag lunges, and wall balls require significant muscular strength. You'll need **functional, full-body strength** rather than just being strong in isolation. Strength training for Hyrox focuses on compound movements, which use multiple muscle groups, mimicking the natural, practical movements used in the event (Bompa & Buzzichelli, 2019).

High-Intensity Circuits

The key to Hyrox is your ability to shift quickly between exercises. High-intensity functional movements like burpee broad jumps and rowing not only test your strength but also demand that you recover and perform well under fatigue. This requires **anaerobic conditioning**, as well as a mental focus to maintain form and speed even when you're exhausted (Bishop et al., 2020).

The **hybrid nature** of Hyrox means that your body needs to be prepared for both long-term endurance and short bursts of power. This balance is what makes Hyrox such a complete fitness test.

Assessing Your Current Fitness Level

Before you start training for Hyrox, it's important to know where you're starting from. Assessing your current fitness level will help you set realistic goals and structure your training plan. Use these benchmarks to get a sense of how prepared you are in three key areas: **running, strength, and cardio-respiratory fitness**.

Running Benchmarks

The running portion of Hyrox is broken into manageable 1K intervals. A good way to assess your readiness is by seeing how fast you can run 1K multiple times with minimal rest. Try running **4 x 1K intervals** with a 2-minute rest in between, aiming to keep a consistent pace throughout each interval. For beginners, shooting for 5:30 to 6:00 per kilometer is a good baseline, while more advanced athletes should aim for under 4:30 per kilometer.

Strength Benchmarks

Hyrox strength stations, like the sled push/pull, require more than just brute force—they demand sustained muscular endurance. Test yourself with these **strength benchmarks**:

- **Sled Push:** Aim to push a sled loaded with at least 70-80% of your body weight for 50 meters.

- **Farmers Carry:** Test your grip and core strength by carrying two kettlebells (24-32 kg for men, 16-24 kg for women) for 100 meters without dropping them.

- **Wall Balls:** Can you complete **50 consecutive wall balls** (20 lbs for men, 14 lbs for women) without stopping?

Cardio-Respiratory Fitness Benchmarks

Cardio is the backbone of your performance. To test your endurance, try completing a **2,000-meter row** and aim for times under 8 minutes if you're an experienced athlete or around 9:30 for beginners. Another good test is the **15-minute burpee challenge**: how many burpees can you complete in 15 minutes? Anything over 100 is a strong result.

By performing these tests, you'll get a clearer idea of your strengths and weaknesses, and you can tailor your training program accordingly.

Setting Realistic Goals Based on Your Fitness Baseline

Once you've assessed your fitness, it's time to set goals. **Goal setting** is crucial in structuring your training and ensuring you stay motivated. The key is to be **realistic yet ambitious**.

Beginner Goals

If you're new to fitness or have never participated in a functional fitness event before, your goals should focus on building a solid foundation in both **cardiovascular endurance and functional strength**. Your initial aim should be to **complete the Hyrox event** rather than focusing on a specific time. Gradually increase the intensity and volume of your training while allowing time for recovery.

Intermediate Goals

Athletes with some experience in running or strength training can aim for more specific performance markers. For instance, set a goal to complete the event in **under 90 minutes**, with targets for each station (e.g., 4 minutes for sled push/pull, 5 minutes for wall balls).

Advanced Goals

Experienced athletes who already have a solid fitness base should focus on **fine-tuning their performance**. This might mean shaving seconds off each kilometer or station. An advanced goal could be to **complete Hyrox in under 75 minutes** or place in the top 10% in your age group. These athletes may focus on optimizing transitions between stations and reducing time wasted on recovery during the event.

Research shows that **goal-setting** can significantly improve performance by providing a clear target and motivation to work toward it (Locke & Latham, 2002). The important thing is to make your goals specific, measurable, and achievable based on your current fitness level.

Key Takeaways

- Hyrox requires a balance of endurance, strength, and high-intensity performance.
- Assessing your fitness through benchmarks in running, strength, and cardio will give you a baseline to create a personalized training plan.
- Setting realistic, progressive goals based on your current fitness level will help you structure your training and improve your performance.

Chapter 3: The Science of Functional Fitness

When it comes to Hyrox, training for functional fitness is the foundation of success. Unlike traditional fitness routines that may focus exclusively on strength or endurance, Hyrox challenges your body to excel at both. This chapter explores the delicate balance between strength and endurance, the role of muscle fiber types, and why functional fitness is crucial for dominating the event.

Understanding the Balance Between Strength and Endurance

One of the unique aspects of Hyrox is that it requires athletes to be well-rounded—capable of running multiple kilometers while also performing power-driven movements like sled pushes and wall balls. This duality is where the concept of **functional fitness** truly shines, allowing you to adapt to a range of challenges in a real-world or competitive setting (Calatayud et al., 2015).

Strength and **endurance** are often viewed as opposing forces, but in functional fitness, they work hand-in-hand. For instance, during Hyrox, after running a kilometer, you immediately switch to high-intensity strength stations. This switch demands a combination of **muscular endurance** (your ability to maintain force output over time) and **cardiovascular endurance** (your heart and lungs' ability to sustain prolonged activity).

The key to success lies in the **hybridization of these qualities**. A strong athlete who lacks endurance may struggle with running or sustaining high-rep exercises, while an endurance athlete with insufficient strength may face difficulty in pushing or pulling a heavy sled. A well-balanced Hyrox athlete thrives in both domains, and functional training provides this balance by emphasizing movement patterns that improve **stamina, power, and overall durability** (Schoenfeld et al., 2015).

Muscle Fiber Types: Fast-Twitch vs. Slow-Twitch and Their Role in Hyrox

Your muscles are made up of different types of fibers—**slow-twitch (Type I)** and **fast-twitch (Type II)**—and they play a crucial role in determining your performance in both endurance and strength activities.

- **Slow-Twitch (Type I) Fibers:**

These muscle fibers are responsible for **endurance activities**. They generate force slowly but are highly resistant to fatigue, making them ideal for long-distance running and aerobic exercises. In Hyrox, slow-twitch fibers help you maintain a steady pace during the 8K run, as well as provide the stamina for repeated, lower-intensity exercises like the rowing portion.

- **Fast-Twitch (Type II) Fibers:**

These fibers are designed for **power and speed**. Fast-twitch muscles can contract quickly and generate a large amount of force, but they fatigue much faster than slow-twitch fibers. This makes them perfect for short bursts of high-intensity efforts, like sled pushes or explosive exercises such as burpee broad jumps. Fast-twitch fibers are key for executing the strength-based movements in Hyrox efficiently (Zatsiorsky & Kraemer, 2006).

Most athletes have a genetic predisposition toward one fiber type, but functional fitness training can help improve your performance in both areas by teaching your body to better recruit these fibers. Functional movements, such as squats or kettlebell swings, challenge both muscle fiber types, allowing for a better **balance between power and endurance**—a critical factor in Hyrox success (Sale, 1988).

Why Functional Fitness Training is Crucial for Optimal Hyrox Performance

Functional fitness focuses on **movements** that mirror the challenges your body faces in everyday life, such as squatting, pulling, lifting, and running. In Hyrox, these same movement patterns are crucial for success. Functional fitness is more than just lifting weights or running on a treadmill; it's about preparing your body to perform in dynamic environments, which is why it's a perfect training method for this event.

Here are three reasons functional fitness is key to your Hyrox preparation:

1. It Develops Multidimensional Strength:

Unlike bodybuilding, which isolates muscle groups, functional fitness builds strength through compound movements that involve multiple joints and muscles. These exercises help develop the **total-body strength** needed for tasks like the sled push/pull or sandbag lunges, where both upper- and lower-body strength are engaged simultaneously (Boyle, 2016).

2. It Enhances Your Core and Stability:

Almost every exercise in Hyrox—whether it's rowing, carrying a farmer's load, or performing burpees—requires a strong core. Functional fitness drills like planks, kettlebell carries, or deadlifts improve **core stability**, which helps in maintaining good form, reducing injury risk, and efficiently transferring power during strength stations (Behm & Anderson, 2006).

3. It Builds Endurance for High-Intensity Efforts:

Hyrox is all about performing at high intensity, and functional fitness helps prepare your body for this through circuits, intervals, and compound exercises that blend strength and endurance. These movements improve your **muscular endurance** and ability to recover quickly, which are essential for transitioning smoothly between running and strength stations without losing steam.

Key Takeaways

- Hyrox is a unique event that requires athletes to excel in both endurance and strength, and functional fitness provides the foundation to train both qualities effectively.

- Muscle fiber types—fast-twitch and slow-twitch—play specific roles in Hyrox, influencing your ability to perform under different intensities. Functional fitness helps improve both.

- Functional fitness training is essential because it develops multidimensional strength, enhances core stability, and builds the endurance needed for high-intensity efforts.

Chapter 4: Your 12-Week Training Plan

In this chapter, we'll lay out a structured 12-week training plan designed to prepare you for Hyrox success. Whether you're a beginner, intermediate, or advanced athlete, this plan will guide you step-by-step, combining the right amount of **running**, **strength training**, and **recovery** to ensure you peak at the right time. Hyrox is a unique event, and the goal here is to enhance your functional fitness, build your stamina, and help you master the specific skills required for each stage of the competition.

It is important to point out that as Hyrox is a quite new sport, nobody knows exactly the best way to train for it. However, we do have a very good understanding based on functional fitness and cardio training, but we are sure that new and better ways of training for Hyrox will be discovered as this sport grows.

Overview of the 12-Week Progressive Training Plan

The key to a successful training program for Hyrox is **progression**. Over the course of 12 weeks, you will gradually increase the intensity and volume of your workouts to optimize your strength and endurance without overtraining.

- **Weeks 1-4**: Building a base. In these first weeks, you'll focus on **improving endurance** through steady-state runs and light strength work. The goal is to establish a solid foundation while learning to integrate functional movements.
- **Weeks 5-8**: Hyrox-specific skills. This phase shifts to **combining strength and cardio** through high-intensity interval training (HIIT), resistance training, and event-specific exercises like sled pushes and farmer's carries.
- **Weeks 9-12**: Peaking and tapering. The final weeks are all about **maximizing your performance**, incorporating simulated Hyrox events, and then tapering down to ensure you are rested and ready for race day.

Throughout the plan, you'll alternate between **strength training**, **cardio (running)**, and **functional movements** tailored to Hyrox. This progressive approach ensures that your body adapts without injury, gradually improving both your **aerobic capacity** and **muscular endurance** (Rhea et al., 2003).

Week-by-Week Breakdown

Weeks 1-4: Build Your Base

Objective: Increase aerobic capacity and introduce functional movements.

- **Running**: 3-4 runs per week, focusing on low-intensity, steady-state efforts to improve aerobic endurance. Start with 30-40 minutes at a moderate pace, gradually building up to 60 minutes.

- **Strength Training**: 2-3 sessions per week, focusing on **compound movements** (squats, deadlifts, and lunges) with lighter weights and higher reps (3-4 sets of 10-12 reps). These movements build the foundation for functional fitness.

- **Functional Movements**: Incorporate **planks, kettlebell swings, and farmer's carries** to start conditioning your body for the functional tasks you'll face in Hyrox.

Weeks 5-8: Hyrox Skills and High-Intensity Training

Objective: Increase intensity, introduce event-specific exercises, and build muscular endurance.

- **Running**: 2-3 steady-state runs and 1 **interval training session** per week. Your interval training should include sprint efforts (like 400-meter repeats) followed by active recovery.

- **Strength Training**: Focus on **strength endurance**—using moderate weights with shorter rest periods (4-5 sets of 8-10 reps). Exercises like sled pushes, wall balls, and deadlifts mimic the demands of the Hyrox event (Häkkinen et al., 2003).

- **Functional Movements**: Begin adding **sled pushes/pulls**, **burpee broad jumps**, and **rower sprints** into your routine. Each week, increase the volume and intensity to replicate Hyrox race conditions.

Weeks 9-12: Race Simulation and Taper

Objective: Simulate race conditions and ensure optimal recovery before the event.

- **Running**: Cut back on steady-state runs to allow more recovery. Continue with **interval training** and add **longer race-paced efforts** (such as 5-6km at Hyrox pace).

- **Strength Training**: Simulate the race by performing **circuit-style workouts** combining strength and endurance exercises (i.e., 1km run followed by sled pushes, wall balls, etc.). Focus on maintaining intensity while managing fatigue.

- **Functional Movements**: Replicate the entire Hyrox race structure during your training sessions (8x 1km runs + corresponding strength movements) to practice transitions and pacing. In the final week, taper down to allow full recovery for race day.

Modifying the Plan Based on Fitness Level

No two athletes are the same, and your training plan should reflect your unique fitness level. Here's how you can modify the 12-week program to suit your needs:

- **Beginner**: If you're new to Hyrox or functional fitness, focus on building a strong foundation with **lighter weights** and **shorter runs**. Aim for 2-3 training days per week with extra rest days, gradually increasing volume and intensity.

- **Intermediate**: Athletes with a good fitness base can handle **4-5 training sessions per week**, with a higher focus on **combining running and strength**. Start incorporating **interval training** and **Hyrox-specific movements** earlier in the plan.

- **Advanced**: Experienced athletes can fine-tune their performance by integrating **high-intensity interval training (HIIT)** and **simulated Hyrox events** from the start. Aim for 5-6 training days per week, paying special attention to recovery strategies.

Remember, while it's important to follow a structured plan, **listen to your body** and adjust as needed. If you're feeling overly fatigued, it's okay to scale back intensity or take an additional rest day.

Key Takeaways

- The 12-week Hyrox training plan is designed to progressively build your strength, endurance, and race-specific skills.
- The plan is broken into three phases: building a fitness base, increasing intensity with Hyrox-specific exercises, and race simulation with tapering.
- Tailor the plan based on your fitness level to avoid burnout and maximize race-day performance.

Chapter 5: Strength Workouts for Hyrox

Strength training is the backbone of your Hyrox performance. Each event challenge—from sled pushes to wall balls—requires a blend of **muscular strength**, **power**, and **endurance**. In this chapter, we'll dive into specific exercises that will prepare you for each Hyrox station, while also ensuring your body is ready to handle the rigors of race day.

The key to success in Hyrox is focusing on **functional strength**. This means performing exercises that mimic the movements you'll face during the event, all while incorporating **progressive overload** to ensure your muscles adapt and grow stronger over time.

Specific Exercises to Build Strength for Hyrox Challenges

To perform well in Hyrox, you need to develop strength in key areas: upper body, lower body, and core. Below are some essential exercises to include in your training routine, each targeting specific aspects of the event.

1. Sled Pushes and Pulls

- **Target**: Full body (legs, glutes, back, core, arms).
- **Why**: The sled push and pull is one of the most grueling sections of Hyrox. It requires immense lower body strength and endurance, but your upper body and core also play a significant role in stabilizing and generating power.
- **How**: Push a loaded sled across a 15-20 meter distance, focusing on maintaining a low, athletic stance. Increase the weight and distance over time to build both power and endurance.
- Video for Sled Push: IMPROVE your Sled Push for HYROX / Top P...

- Video for Sled Pulls: How to MASTER Sled Pulls for HYROX / Top...

2. Wall Balls

- **Target**: Legs, glutes, shoulders, core.
- **Why**: The wall ball station involves squatting with a weighted ball and then launching it up to a target. It's a combination of leg power and upper body strength, along with cardiovascular endurance.
- **How**: Start with a lighter ball (6-9kg) and aim for 15-20 repetitions, focusing on explosive power as you stand and throw. As you progress, increase the weight of the ball and number of reps to improve both strength and endurance.
- Video for Wall Balls: HYROX Wall Ball Top Tips W/ George Edwards

3. Farmer's Carries

- **Target**: Grip strength, traps, core, legs.
- **Why**: Grip endurance and core stability are crucial during the farmer's carry. Carrying heavy loads over a distance challenges your entire body, especially your forearms, traps, and core.

- **How**: Hold a heavy dumbbell or kettlebell in each hand and walk for 50-100 meters. As your strength improves, increase the weight or distance.
- Video for Farmer's Carries: ▶ How To Get QUICKER at Farmers Walk for H...

4. Burpee Broad Jumps

- **Target**: Chest, shoulders, legs, core.
- **Why**: This movement combines the explosive power of a broad jump with the functional strength required for burpees. It builds overall body power and endurance.
- **How**: Perform a burpee and, as you come up, immediately transition into a broad jump. Focus on explosive movements and proper form. Start with 10-12 repetitions and increase over time.
- Video for Burpee Broad Jumps: ▶ Get The CORRECT Burpee Broad Jump Form ...

5. Deadlifts

- **Target**: Hamstrings, glutes, lower back, core.
- **Why**: Deadlifts are crucial for building the posterior chain strength needed for many Hyrox movements, including sled pulls and rowing.
- **How**: Begin with a moderate weight and perform 3-4 sets of 8-10 repetitions. Over time, increase the weight as you develop strength in your hamstrings, glutes, and lower back.
- Video for Deadlifts: ▶ The Deadlift

6. Rowing Intervals

- **Target**: Full body (legs, back, shoulders, core).
- **Why**: Rowing is both a strength and endurance challenge in Hyrox. You need strong legs and back muscles to generate power efficiently.
- **How**: Incorporate intervals into your training, such as 250-500 meters at maximum effort, followed by a short rest. This will help build both power and stamina for the rowing portion of Hyrox.

- Video for Rowing: ▶ Rowing Technique Tips

Workout Variations to Target Upper Body, Lower Body, and Core

Hyrox is a full-body challenge, so your strength training should reflect that by dividing your workouts into **upper body**, **lower body**, and **core-focused** sessions.

Upper Body Workouts

- **Push Movements**: Focus on exercises like **bench presses**, **push-ups**, and **overhead presses**. These will help with sled pushes and wall ball throws.
- **Pull Movements**: Incorporate **pull-ups**, **rows**, and **deadlifts** to strengthen the muscles needed for sled pulls, rowing, and grip-based events like the farmer's carry.

Lower Body Workouts

- **Squats**: Variations like **back squats** and **front squats** will improve your power for wall balls and lunges. Start with lighter weights and higher reps, progressing to heavier loads.
- **Lunges**: Forward or walking lunges will strengthen your quads and glutes, which are key in nearly every Hyrox event.
- **Box Jumps**: Incorporating plyometric movements like box jumps will improve your explosiveness, especially useful for the burpee broad jump.

Core Workouts

- **Planks**: Static and dynamic planks will enhance your core stability, which is crucial for sled pulls, farmer's carries, and overall strength endurance.
- **Russian Twists**: These help build rotational strength, which supports functional movements like sled pulls.
- **Kettlebell Swings**: These combine core strength with explosive power, useful for both cardiovascular endurance and functional strength.

Incorporating Progressive Overload to Ensure Continual Improvement

The principle of **progressive overload** means gradually increasing the **intensity**, **volume**, or **weight** in your workouts to keep your body adapting and improving. Here's how to apply this concept in your Hyrox strength training:

- **Increase Weight**: As you grow stronger, incrementally increase the weight for exercises like deadlifts, squats, and farmer's carries. Aim for a 5-10% increase every 1-2 weeks.

- **Increase Reps**: If increasing the weight is not feasible, work on adding more repetitions to your sets. For example, if you can comfortably perform 3 sets of 8 reps, aim to do 10-12 reps next week.

- **Increase Volume**: Add more sets or reduce rest times between sets to further challenge your body and improve endurance. For instance, start with 3 sets per exercise and build up to 4-5 sets as you progress.

Key Takeaways

- Specific strength exercises like sled pushes, wall balls, and farmer's carries are essential for Hyrox performance.

- Workout variations targeting upper body, lower body, and core will create a balanced and functional strength base.
- Using progressive overload ensures continual improvement, helping you get stronger and more conditioned over time.

Chapter 6: Running Workouts for Endurance and Speed

When it comes to Hyrox, running plays a critical role, accounting for 8 kilometers of the event, broken into 1-kilometer intervals between the functional fitness stations. That's a significant portion of your race! To excel, you need a balance of **endurance** and **speed**. This chapter will focus on how to build both through a well-rounded running plan.

Running isn't just about covering distance—it's about doing so with the strength and stamina to seamlessly transition into and out of physically demanding challenges like the sled push or farmer's carry. Let's break down the key types of running workouts that will prepare you for Hyrox, as well as tips on combining running and strength training.

Interval Training, Tempo Runs, and Long-Distance Running: Their Roles in Hyrox Preparation

Your running workouts need variety to prepare for both the fast sprints between stations and the endurance required to maintain pace across 8 kilometers. Here's a look at the three core types of running workouts to include in your training:

1. Interval Training

- **Why**: Interval training involves alternating periods of high-intensity running with rest or lower-intensity effort. This type of workout increases your **VO2 max** (your body's ability to use oxygen efficiently), which is crucial for the fast-paced nature of Hyrox.
- **How**: Perform intervals like 400m sprints at 90-95% of your maximum effort, followed by 1-2 minutes of walking or jogging for recovery. Start with 6-8 repeats and gradually increase the intensity and number of intervals as your fitness improves.
- **Example Workout**: 400m sprints x 8 (90% effort), with 90 seconds of walking recovery in between.

2. Tempo Runs

- **Why**: Tempo runs are steady-state runs performed at a "comfortably hard" pace—typically about 80-85% of your maximum heart rate. They are designed to improve your **lactate threshold**, helping you maintain a faster pace for longer periods without fatiguing.

- **How**: Start with shorter tempo runs, around 15-20 minutes, at a pace just below your 10K race pace. Gradually increase the duration to 30-40 minutes as you progress.
- **Example Workout**: 20-minute tempo run at a pace that feels challenging but sustainable for the duration.

3. Long-Distance Running

- **Why**: Long-distance runs build your **aerobic endurance** and mental toughness, helping you maintain your form and composure during the longer stretches of the race. They also help condition your body to handle the accumulated fatigue of running 8 kilometers.
- **How**: Start with a weekly long run at an easy, conversational pace. Increase the distance by about 10% each week, aiming for runs between 10-12 kilometers as you approach race day.
- **Example Workout**: 10K long run at an easy pace, focusing on consistency rather than speed.

Pacing Strategies for Race Day

One of the most common mistakes athletes make during Hyrox is going out too fast at the start of the race. Given that you'll be transitioning between high-intensity functional movements and running, pacing is crucial to avoid early burnout.

Pacing Tips:

1. **Negative Splits**: Start conservatively and gradually increase your pace over time. Your goal is to finish the last kilometer faster than the first.
2. **Run by Effort, Not Just Pace**: Given the variability of your heart rate and energy levels during transitions, it's better to run by how you feel rather than sticking strictly to a predetermined pace.
3. **Recover on the Runs**: Use the running segments as an opportunity to recover slightly after the more taxing functional stations. Focus on maintaining a steady, controlled pace.

Example Pacing Strategy:

- **Kilometers 1-3**: Aim to run at 70-75% effort, keeping a steady but comfortable pace.
- **Kilometers 4-6**: Increase to 80-85% effort as you settle into the race.

- **Kilometers 7-8**: Push to 90-95% effort, finishing strong.

How to Combine Strength Training and Running Without Overtraining

Hyrox demands both running endurance and functional strength, but balancing these without overtraining can be tricky. The key is smart programming: integrating strength and running workouts in a way that maximizes recovery and prevents burnout.

1. Schedule Smartly

- **Alternate Days**: Ideally, alternate between running and strength-focused days. For example, after a day of heavy leg work (e.g., sled pushes, squats), opt for an upper-body strength session or an easy recovery run the following day.
- **Double Sessions**: For athletes with limited time, consider double sessions—running in the morning and strength training in the evening. Ensure one session is high-intensity while the other is more recovery-focused to avoid excessive fatigue.

2. Prioritize Recovery

- **Rest Days**: Incorporate at least one complete rest day per week, especially after intense training blocks.

- **Active Recovery**: Use lower-intensity activities like walking, swimming, or yoga on active recovery days to promote blood flow and muscle repair without taxing your body.

3. Listen to Your Body

- **Adjust Workouts Based on Fatigue**: If you feel unusually fatigued or sore, adjust your training. Reduce the intensity or duration of your workouts to allow your body more time to recover.

Key Takeaways

- Incorporate a variety of running workouts—intervals, tempo runs, and long-distance runs—to build both speed and endurance for Hyrox.
- Pacing is essential on race day; starting too fast can lead to burnout, so focus on negative splits and effort-based running.
- Balancing strength training and running requires smart scheduling and a focus on recovery to avoid overtraining and injury.

Chapter 7: Hyrox-Specific Workouts

Training for Hyrox isn't just about building strength or improving your running endurance—it's about developing the specific skills and efficiency to tackle each of the event's functional fitness challenges. In this chapter, we'll explore workouts tailored specifically to the demands of Hyrox, designed to help you excel in key movements like the sled push, rowing, and burpee broad jumps, while also incorporating hybrid sessions that blend strength and running for optimal race preparation.

Circuit Training that Mimics Hyrox Challenges

Circuit training is a cornerstone of Hyrox preparation because it allows you to replicate race conditions by stringing together functional exercises with minimal rest, much like you'll encounter during the event. These circuits should target both **strength** and **conditioning**, and can be adjusted to your current fitness level.

Example Hyrox Circuit:

1. **Sled Push (50 meters)**
   - Focus on explosive lower body power and technique. Drive through your legs, keeping your body low to the sled. Mimicking the 202.5kg sled weight used in Hyrox, gradually increase the load over time.

2. **Burpee Broad Jumps (20 meters)**
   - The burpee broad jump is a full-body movement that taxes your cardiovascular system while engaging your core, legs, and upper body. Focus on controlled, explosive jumps and minimize rest between burpees.

3. **Rowing (1000 meters)**
   - Hyrox includes a 1000m row, so this is a critical element in training. Rowing engages the legs, back, and core, making it essential for both strength and endurance.

4. **Sled Pull (50 meters)**
   - The sled pull requires strong posterior chain engagement (back, hamstrings, glutes). Focus on a consistent, smooth pull using your legs and arms in harmony.

5. **Farmer's Carry (200 meters)**
   - Grip strength, core stability, and mental toughness are tested in this event. Use

kettlebells or dumbbells to mimic the challenge, aiming to build strength gradually.

How to Perform the Circuit:

- **Rest**: After completing all exercises, rest for 2-3 minutes. Repeat the circuit 3-5 times, depending on your fitness level.
- **Intensity**: As you progress, shorten rest times or increase the weights used for the sled and carries to continue challenging your body.

How to Improve Efficiency in Key Movements

Efficiency in each Hyrox movement is what separates the finishers from the top performers. Knowing how to move well not only helps conserve energy but also shaves off valuable time during transitions.

Sled Push and Pull Efficiency:

- **Technique Tips**: Keep your core tight and use your legs to generate power. For the sled push, lean into the sled with your shoulders, creating a more efficient angle for maximal force application. With the sled pull, focus on pulling with your legs first and then your arms to avoid fatigue in your upper body early on. (Refer to Chapter 5 to see video on tips for these exercises)

Rowing Efficiency:

- **Technique Tips**: Rowing in Hyrox isn't about speed; it's about maintaining consistent power output. Focus on long, powerful strokes and avoid excessive upper body involvement to conserve strength for later in the race. Practice rowing at your race pace in training to build muscle memory and efficiency. (Refer to Chapter 5 to see video on tips for these exercises)

Burpee Broad Jump Efficiency:

- **Technique Tips**: A well-executed burpee can save both time and energy. Keep your jumps controlled and land softly to protect your knees and avoid injury. Transition smoothly between the burpee and broad jump portions by keeping your body in motion without sacrificing form. (Refer to Chapter 5 to see video on tips for these exercises)

Farmer's Carry Efficiency:

- **Technique Tips**: Grip strength plays a huge role here, so make sure to practice holding weights for extended periods without dropping them. When moving, stay upright and engage your core to stabilize the load, using short, controlled steps. (Refer to Chapter 5 to see video on tips for these exercises)

Integrating Hybrid Sessions that Combine Strength and Running

One of the most challenging aspects of Hyrox is transitioning from functional movements (like the sled push or rowing) to running. Hybrid sessions that combine both elements into a single workout will help prepare your body for these demanding transitions.

Hybrid Workout Example:

1. **1K Run at Race Pace**
   - After completing a functional movement station, run at a controlled but challenging pace. This will simulate the transition between stations and build endurance.
2. **Sled Push (20 meters)**
   - Keep the sled heavy to mimic race conditions. Focus on maintaining good form and explosiveness.
3. **Row (500 meters)**
   - Row at a moderate pace, concentrating on consistent power output.
4. **Burpee Broad Jumps (10 meters)**
   - Use this movement to develop cardiovascular endurance and explosive leg power.
5. **Rest 2-3 minutes and repeat the cycle 3-4 times.**

Key Takeaways

- Circuit training is a vital part of Hyrox preparation, as it replicates the race environment and conditions.
- Efficiency in key Hyrox movements (sled push, burpee broad jumps, rowing) can make a significant difference in overall performance.
- Incorporating hybrid workouts that combine strength and running will help prepare you for the unique demands of Hyrox and improve your race day endurance.

Chapter 8: Nutrition for Hyrox Athletes

When it comes to Hyrox, nutrition is just as critical as your training. A well-balanced diet fuels your performance, aids in recovery, and ensures you can push through both the strength and endurance aspects of the event. In this chapter, we'll break down how to optimize your macronutrient intake, pre-race nutrition, hydration strategies, and supplements that can help enhance your strength, endurance, and recovery.

Macronutrient Breakdown: Fueling for Performance

Hyrox demands a balance of strength and endurance, which means your diet needs to support both muscular power and long-duration stamina. The key macronutrients—**carbohydrates, proteins, and fats**—each play a unique role in preparing your body to perform at its best.

Carbohydrates: Your Primary Energy Source

For endurance events like Hyrox, carbohydrates are essential. Carbs are broken down into glucose, which fuels your muscles during high-intensity efforts. Whether you're pushing a sled or sprinting between stations, carbs provide the quick-access energy you need to perform.

- **Daily intake**: Aim for around **4-6 grams per kilogram of body weight** on training days (Jeukendrup & Gleeson, 2018). As race day approaches, increasing this to **6-8 grams per kilogram** will ensure glycogen stores are topped off for sustained energy.

Proteins: Muscle Repair and Growth

Functional strength is a core component of Hyrox, and your muscles will undergo significant wear and tear during training. Adequate protein intake ensures that your body can repair muscle tissue and build strength.

- **Daily intake**: For athletes, a target of **1.6-2.2 grams per kilogram of body weight** per day is optimal for muscle repair and recovery (Jäger et al., 2017). Focus on high-quality protein sources such as lean meats, fish, eggs, and plant-based proteins like tofu and legumes.

Fats: Sustained Energy

While carbs are key for high-intensity efforts, fats provide a longer-lasting fuel source, especially for the endurance portions of the race. Healthy fats, particularly **omega-3 fatty acids**, also reduce inflammation and support recovery.

- **Daily intake**: Aim for **20-30% of your total caloric intake** to come from fats, with an emphasis on sources like avocados, nuts, seeds, olive oil, and fatty fish (Sahlin, 2014).

Pre-Race Nutrition and Hydration Strategies

Your nutrition strategy in the days leading up to the event can make or break your performance on race day. Here's how to fuel up for success:

Carbohydrate Loading

In the 2-3 days before the event, it's time to increase your carb intake to ensure your muscle glycogen stores are fully replenished. Stick with easy-to-digest carbs such as rice, pasta, sweet potatoes, and fruits to avoid digestive discomfort.

- ❖ **Carb-loading tip**: Combine carbs with small amounts of protein to stabilize blood sugar levels and avoid energy crashes.

Hydration

Proper hydration is essential for both strength and endurance. Dehydration can lead to impaired performance, especially during the longer runs and high-intensity circuits. Aim to stay fully hydrated in the 48 hours before race day.

❖ **Race-day tip**: On race morning, drink about **500ml of water** 2-3 hours before the start. During the race, sip water at hydration stations to stay ahead of any fluid loss.

Pre-Race Meal

Eat a balanced, easily digestible meal 2-3 hours before the race. A mix of carbohydrates and proteins works well, such as oatmeal with banana and peanut butter or a turkey sandwich on whole-grain bread.

❖ **Avoid**: High-fat and high-fiber foods, as they may cause stomach discomfort during the race.

Supplements that Support Endurance, Strength, and Recovery

While a well-rounded diet should provide most of the nutrients you need, supplements can be helpful in giving you an extra edge. Let's explore the most beneficial supplements for Hyrox athletes.

Creatine Monohydrate

One of the most researched supplements in the sports industry is creatine. This supplement can increase your explosive power, which is crucial for movements like sled pushes and farmer's carries (Kreider et al., 2017).

❖ **Dosage**: **3-5 grams per day** taken consistently will help improve strength, power output, and muscle endurance.

Beta-Alanine

Beta-alanine helps buffer the lactic acid build-up in your muscles, delaying fatigue during high-intensity efforts like burpee broad jumps or rowing (Hobson et al., 2012).

❖ **Dosage**: **2-5 grams per day** will help reduce muscle fatigue during longer efforts.

Caffeine

Caffeine is well-known for improving focus, energy, and endurance. Consuming caffeine 30-60 minutes before your event can help you stay mentally sharp and physically energized throughout the race (Grgic et al., 2019).

❖ **Dosage**: Aim for **3-6 mg per kilogram of body weight** for optimal performance.

Electrolytes

Replenishing lost electrolytes, particularly **sodium, potassium, and magnesium**, is crucial to maintaining proper muscle function during long and intense workouts.

❖ **Race-day tip**: Use an electrolyte drink or supplement during the race to avoid cramping and fatigue.

Key Takeaways

- Carbohydrates are your primary energy source for high-intensity movements in Hyrox. Ensure you're adequately fueled with 4-6 grams per kilogram of body weight, increasing before race day.
- Protein is crucial for muscle repair and recovery. Aim for 1.6-2.2 grams per kilogram of body weight daily.
- Pre-race nutrition should focus on easily digestible carbohydrates and hydration, with an emphasis on carbohydrate loading in the days leading up to the event.
- Supplements such as creatine, beta-alanine, caffeine, and electrolytes can give you an extra performance edge when used appropriately.

Chapter 9: Mental Toughness and Motivation

In a Hyrox race, your body will undoubtedly be pushed to its limits. But what often separates a successful athlete from an unsuccessful one is not just physical conditioning, but mental toughness. The ability to stay focused, push through discomfort, and maintain motivation is key to your performance on race day. In this chapter, we'll explore how to build mental resilience, push past your breaking points, and stay motivated through visualization and goal-setting techniques.

The Importance of Mindset in Hyrox Success

While physical strength and endurance are crucial, the right mindset is what allows you to unlock your true potential during a race. As fatigue sets in, negative thoughts can creep in, tempting you to slow down or stop altogether. Athletes who have a strong mindset can override these thoughts and maintain performance even when their bodies are fatigued.

Growth vs. Fixed Mindset

Psychologist Carol Dweck's research on mindset shows that athletes with a **growth mindset**—the belief that abilities can be developed through hard work and perseverance—are more likely to overcome setbacks and challenges (Dweck, 2016). In contrast, those with a **fixed mindset** may view difficulties as a reflection of their limits and become discouraged.

- ❖ **Growth mindset tip**: Frame every challenge, whether it's a difficult training session or a tough section of the race, as an opportunity to grow stronger and improve. Celebrate small wins, and use failures as stepping stones for future success.

Building Resilience: How to Push Through the Toughest Parts of the Race

Resilience is your ability to stay mentally strong when the going gets tough—an essential skill for Hyrox athletes. Whether you're struggling with the last few meters of a sled push or feel like your legs can't carry you any further, resilience can help you keep moving forward.

Pain vs. Discomfort

Understanding the difference between pain and discomfort is crucial in building resilience. Pain is your body's signal that something might be wrong, while discomfort is simply the natural response to pushing yourself physically and mentally. Elite athletes are often masters at distinguishing between these sensations (Marcora & Staiano, 2010).

❖ **Resilience tip**: When you feel discomfort setting in, use positive self-talk to reframe it as a sign that you're growing stronger, not weaker. Tell yourself, "I've prepared for this," or "This is where I improve."

Breathing Techniques

Controlled breathing can help regulate stress, especially during high-intensity efforts. Research shows that slow, controlled breathing can activate the **parasympathetic nervous system**, reducing your body's stress response and allowing you to maintain focus (Jerath et al., 2015).

❖ **Breathing technique**: Try **box breathing** (inhaling for 4 seconds, holding for 4 seconds, exhaling for 4 seconds, and holding again for 4 seconds) during moments of high intensity or when you're struggling mentally.

Visualization Techniques and Goal Setting for Sustained Motivation

Visualization and goal setting are powerful tools that can help you stay motivated throughout your training and on race day. Elite athletes often use these techniques to mentally rehearse their performances, boost confidence, and stay focused on their objectives.

Visualization: Rehearsing Success

Visualization involves imagining yourself successfully completing your race or workout. Studies suggest that athletes who visualize their performance improve their motivation and confidence, making it easier to execute on race day (Cumming & Ramsey, 2009).

❖ **Visualization exercise**: Close your eyes and imagine yourself performing each part of the Hyrox event. Picture yourself nailing the transitions, maintaining your pace, and crossing the finish line with a strong finish. Use all your senses—how it feels, sounds, and looks—to make the experience as vivid as possible.

SMART Goals

Goal setting helps provide structure and direction to your training. Using **SMART goals**—Specific, Measurable, Achievable, Relevant, and Time-bound—can keep you focused and motivated throughout your journey.

❖ **Goal-setting example**: Instead of setting a vague goal like "I want to finish Hyrox," break it down into more actionable goals, such as "I want to complete the sled pull in under 5 minutes by the end of my 8th week of training." This makes your progress measurable and easier to track.

Key Takeaways

- Mental toughness can make the difference between finishing strong and giving up. Building resilience and having a growth mindset are key to pushing through the toughest parts of the race.

- Learning to distinguish between pain and discomfort is critical. Embrace discomfort as a sign of progress, and use positive self-talk to stay focused during difficult moments.

- Visualization and setting SMART goals can help you stay motivated and mentally prepared. Rehearse your race mentally and create achievable goals that guide your training.

Chapter 10: Race Day Strategy

Race day is the culmination of your hard work, training, and dedication. It's not just about physical preparation; mental and strategic aspects play a crucial role in achieving your best performance. In this chapter, we'll discuss how to pace yourself effectively, what essential items to bring along, and how to prepare both mentally and physically before you step onto that starting line.

Pacing Yourself Through the Eight Workout Stations and Running Segments

Understanding the Hyrox race format is key to effective pacing. With eight workout stations interspersed with running segments, you must balance your energy to perform well across all tasks. Each segment demands a different focus, so your pacing strategy should adapt accordingly.

Establishing a Rhythm

During the running segments, aim to find a comfortable yet challenging pace. It's crucial not to sprint out of the gates, as this can lead to early fatigue. A good rule of thumb is to run at about 70-80% of your maximum effort for the first half of the race, allowing you to maintain enough energy for the stations that follow (González-Millán et al., 2019).

Workout Station Strategies

At each workout station, focus on maintaining proper form and technique over speed. While it might be tempting to rush through each exercise, doing so can compromise your performance and lead to injury. Instead, aim for a consistent pace across each station and utilize your energy efficiently. For example:

- **Sled Push**: Maintain a steady pace and focus on your leg drive.
- **Rowing**: Keep your strokes controlled, focusing on both power and recovery.
- **Burpee Broad Jumps**: Execute them deliberately to preserve energy for the final running segments.

By maintaining a steady effort and allowing your heart rate to recover slightly during the workout stations, you'll find that you can sustain your performance throughout the race.

What to Bring to the Race: Gear, Nutrition, and Hydration

Preparation extends beyond training; having the right gear, nutrition, and hydration strategy can significantly impact your performance on race day.

Essential Gear

- **Footwear**: Choose running shoes that provide a balance between cushioning and support for the varied demands of Hyrox. Many pro Hyrox athletes are using running shoes with carbon fiber plate to gain extra speed but with enough grip to be able to perform the functional exercises.
- **Clothing**: Wear moisture-wicking, breathable fabrics to keep you comfortable during the race. Layering may also be beneficial if temperatures vary.
- **Accessories**: Consider wearing a good-quality headband or hat to keep sweat out of your eyes, as well as gloves for exercises that may require grip.

Nutrition and Hydration

- **Pre-Race Meal**: As mentioned in more detail on chapter 8, aim for a carbohydrate-rich meal about 2-3 hours before the race. Foods like oatmeal, bananas, or a sports drink can provide the energy needed to fuel your performance (Jeukendrup, 2017).

- **Hydration**: Ensure you're adequately hydrated before the race. Drinking enough water in the days leading up to the event can help optimize your performance. A general guideline is to consume about 500-600 mL of water in the 2-3 hours before the race starts (Sawka et al., 2007).

Pre-Race Warm-Up Routine and Mental Preparation Tips

A proper warm-up routine not only prepares your body but also gets you in the right mindset for the race. Aim to start your warm-up about 20-30 minutes before your start time.

Warm-Up Routine

- **Dynamic Stretching**: Focus on movements that mimic the exercises you'll perform during the race. Include leg swings, lunges, and arm circles.
- **Activation Exercises**: Perform bodyweight exercises like squats, lunges, and push-ups to engage your muscles.
- **Short Runs**: Finish with a light jog for about 5-10 minutes to elevate your heart rate.

Mental Preparation

- **Visualization**: Take a moment to visualize yourself successfully completing the race. Imagine overcoming challenges and crossing the finish line strong. This technique has been shown to enhance performance and reduce anxiety (Morris et al., 2021).
- **Positive Self-Talk**: Use affirmations to build confidence. Phrases like "I am strong" or "I am prepared" can help to reinforce a positive mindset.

Key Takeaways

- **Pacing is key**: Manage your energy wisely across running and workout stations for optimal performance.
- **Prepare your gear**: Bring the right footwear, clothing, and hydration/nutrition strategies to support your race day performance.
- **Warm-up and mental prep**: A proper warm-up and mental preparation techniques like visualization and positive self-talk can set the stage for success on race day.

Chapter 11: Common Pitfalls and How to Avoid Them

Embarking on a Hyrox journey is exhilarating, but it's essential to navigate it wisely. In this chapter, we'll discuss common pitfalls that can hinder your performance and how to steer clear of them. We'll focus on overtraining and injury prevention, nutrition mistakes, and strategies for tackling unexpected challenges on race day.

Overtraining and Injury Prevention

Understanding Overtraining

Overtraining occurs when you push your body beyond its ability to recover, leading to fatigue, decreased performance, and a heightened risk of injury (Kreher & Schwartz, 2012). Signs of overtraining include persistent fatigue, mood swings, and declining performance levels. For Hyrox athletes, balancing intense workouts with adequate recovery is crucial.

Strategies to Avoid Overtraining

1. **Listen to Your Body**: Pay attention to signs of fatigue. If you feel overly tired or experience persistent soreness, consider adjusting your training load.

2. **Incorporate Recovery Days**: Schedule regular rest days to allow your muscles to repair. Active recovery, like light walking or yoga, can be beneficial.

3. **Vary Intensity**: Mix high-intensity workouts with lower-intensity sessions. This approach prevents burnout and enhances recovery (Mujika & Padilla, 2000).

Injury Prevention

Hyrox involves a unique blend of running and functional fitness exercises, increasing the risk of injuries if not executed properly. Common injuries include strains, sprains, and joint pain.

Tips for Injury Prevention

- **Focus on Form**: Prioritize proper technique in all exercises, particularly during high-impact movements like sled pushes or burpee broad jumps.
- **Gradual Progression**: Increase your training intensity and volume gradually to allow your body to adapt.
- **Strengthen Stabilizing Muscles**: Incorporate exercises that target stabilizing muscles to enhance

overall strength and reduce injury risk (Anderson et al., 2015).

Nutrition Mistakes That Could Hurt Your Performance

Nutrition plays a pivotal role in your training and performance. Poor dietary choices can lead to fatigue, reduced strength, and slower recovery.

Common Nutrition Mistakes

1. **Neglecting Carbohydrates**: Carbs are your body's primary energy source. Failing to consume enough can leave you feeling drained during workouts and races (Jeukendrup, 2017).

2. **Ignoring Hydration**: Dehydration can significantly impact performance. Many athletes underestimate their fluid needs, particularly during intense training sessions. Aim to drink enough fluids throughout the day and monitor your hydration status (Sawka et al., 2007).

3. **Inadequate Post-Workout Nutrition**: Failing to replenish nutrients after training can hinder recovery. A post-workout meal or snack should include a mix of carbohydrates and protein to aid muscle repair.

Nutritional Tips

- **Plan Your Meals**: Prepare balanced meals and snacks that include a mix of carbohydrates, proteins, and healthy fats to fuel your training.
- **Stay Consistent**: Consistency in your nutrition habits will optimize your energy levels and recovery.

How to Handle Unexpected Race Day Challenges

Even the best-laid plans can go awry on race day. Unexpected challenges may arise, from fatigue to mental blocks. Preparing for these hurdles can make all the difference.

Dealing with Fatigue

If you find yourself feeling fatigued during the race:

- **Adjust Your Pace**: Slow down if needed. It's better to finish strong than to risk burnout.
- **Focus on Your Breathing**: Implement deep breathing techniques to calm your mind and manage fatigue.

Overcoming Mental Blocks

Mental blocks can derail your performance:

- **Reframe Negative Thoughts**: Instead of thinking, "I can't do this," reframe it to, "I can take this one step at a time."
- **Use Positive Visualization**: Picture yourself succeeding at each stage of the race, which can enhance your motivation and focus.

Key Takeaways

- **Prevent overtraining** by listening to your body, scheduling recovery days, and varying your training intensity.
- **Prioritize proper nutrition** and hydration to optimize your performance and recovery.
- **Prepare for unexpected challenges** on race day by adjusting your pace, focusing on your breathing, and using positive visualization techniques.

Chapter 12: Recovery and Adaptation

Congratulations! You've completed your first Hyrox event, and now it's time to focus on recovery and adaptation. Recovery is a crucial aspect of any training program, especially after a challenging race like Hyrox. In this chapter, we'll explore effective post-race recovery strategies, the role of sleep, hydration, and nutrition in your recovery, and how to modify your training as you move forward.

Post-Race Recovery Strategies

Active Recovery

Active recovery is an essential part of your post-race routine. Instead of plopping down on the couch, engage in light activities that promote blood flow without straining your muscles. Activities like walking, cycling, or swimming can help flush out lactic acid and reduce soreness (Kellmann, 2010). Aim for 20-30 minutes of low-intensity exercise within 24-48 hours after your race.

Stretching and Mobility

Incorporating stretching and mobility work into your recovery regimen is vital. Focus on dynamic stretching post-race to alleviate tightness and enhance flexibility. Consider yoga or foam rolling sessions to target sore muscles and improve your range of motion. Research suggests that regular stretching can improve recovery and performance in athletes (Beck et al., 2018).

Recovery Techniques to Consider

- **Foam Rolling**: Helps relieve muscle tightness and improves circulation.
- **Gentle Yoga**: Enhances flexibility and promotes relaxation.
- **Contrast Baths**: Alternating between hot and cold water can aid in reducing muscle soreness (Higgins et al., 2013).

Sleep, Hydration, and Nutrition for Faster Recovery

The Power of Sleep

Sleep is your body's natural recovery mechanism. During sleep, your body repairs tissues, builds muscle, and strengthens the immune system. Aim for 7-9 hours of quality sleep per night, especially in the days following your race. Research indicates that poor sleep can negatively affect athletic performance and recovery (Walsh et al., 2011).

Hydration

Staying hydrated is crucial for recovery. Replenish lost fluids by drinking water and consuming electrolyte-rich beverages post-race. Monitor your urine color; pale yellow indicates good hydration, while darker colors suggest you need to drink more (Sawka et al., 2007).

Nutrition for Recovery

Proper nutrition is key to effective recovery. Focus on:

- **Protein**: Essential for muscle repair. Aim for 20-30 grams within 30 minutes post-race.
- **Carbohydrates**: Restore glycogen levels. Incorporate whole grains, fruits, and vegetables.
- **Healthy Fats**: Support overall health and inflammation management. Avocados, nuts, and olive oil are excellent sources.

Sample Post-Race Meal

- Grilled chicken with quinoa, steamed broccoli, and a side of mixed berries.

How to Modify Your Training After Completing Your First Hyrox

After completing your first Hyrox, it's essential to adapt your training to continue progressing and avoid burnout. Here's how to modify your approach:

1. **Evaluate Your Performance**: Reflect on what went well and what could be improved. Use your race experience to inform your future training.

2. **Set New Goals**: Now that you have a baseline, consider setting new, achievable goals. These could include improving your time, mastering specific exercises, or participating in another Hyrox event.

3. **Incorporate Deload Weeks**: After intense training cycles, schedule deload weeks where you reduce the volume and intensity of your workouts. This practice aids recovery and prevents overtraining.

4. **Continue Cross-Training**: Maintain a balanced approach to training by incorporating other forms of exercise, such as swimming or cycling, to enhance overall fitness and reduce the risk of injury.

5. **Focus on Weaknesses**: Identify areas for improvement, whether it's strength, speed, or endurance, and design workouts that specifically target those aspects.

Key Takeaways

- **Engage in active recovery** post-race with low-intensity activities to promote blood flow.
- **Prioritize sleep, hydration, and balanced nutrition** to enhance recovery and prepare for future training.
- **Evaluate your performance** after the race and set new goals while incorporating deload weeks to avoid burnout and injuries.

Chapter 13: Advanced Training for Competitive Athletes

As you progress in your Hyrox journey and aim for a podium finish, the need for advanced training techniques becomes paramount. This chapter is tailored for athletes who are committed to refining their skills and improving their performance. Here, we'll delve into specialized training methods, explore advanced strength and endurance techniques, and discuss strategies for breaking through those frustrating plateaus.

How to Train for a Podium Finish

Achieving a podium finish requires a multifaceted approach to training that goes beyond standard workouts. Here are some key components to consider:

1. **Structured Training Plans**: Implement a periodized training plan that cycles through phases of strength, endurance, and specific Hyrox skill work. Periodization helps in maximizing performance while reducing the risk of overtraining (Haff & Nimphius, 2012).

2. **Race Simulation**: Regularly practice race-day conditions by simulating the Hyrox event in your training sessions. This includes performing the workout stations with the running segments in between. Familiarity with the race format will improve your pacing and efficiency during the actual event (Graham et al., 2017).

3. **Focus on Speed and Power**: Include high-intensity interval training (HIIT) and plyometric exercises to develop explosive power and speed. Research indicates that explosive strength is essential for executing movements like sled pushes and burpee broad jumps efficiently (Meyer et al., 2015).

Advanced Strength and Endurance Training Techniques

To enhance your strength and endurance for Hyrox, consider the following advanced training techniques:

1. **Complex Training**: This method involves pairing strength exercises with explosive movements, such as following a heavy deadlift with a set of box jumps. This training style exploits the post-activation potentiation effect, enhancing your power output during subsequent exercises (Tillin & Bishop, 2009).

2. **Metabolic Conditioning**: Incorporate metabolic conditioning workouts to boost your aerobic and anaerobic capacity. These sessions should include

high-rep, low-weight exercises performed at a high intensity with minimal rest. For instance, a circuit combining kettlebell swings, wall balls, and burpees can mimic the demands of Hyrox while improving your work capacity (Coyle, 2004).

3. **Strength-Specific Protocols**: Targeting the specific strength demands of Hyrox events, such as heavy sled pushes and farmer's carries, is crucial. Use exercises like heavy squats, deadlifts, and carries in your training to build the necessary strength. Incorporating progressive overload ensures continual improvement, pushing your limits and preventing stagnation in performance (Haff et al., 2008).

Strategies for Breaking Through Plateaus

Plateaus can be frustrating, but they are a common part of any athlete's journey. Here are strategies to help you push through:

1. **Vary Your Routine**: Change up your workouts by altering your training variables—volume, intensity, rest periods, or exercise selection. This change can stimulate new adaptations and overcome stagnation (Pritchett et al., 2016).

2. **Incorporate Deload Weeks**: Allow your body to recover and adapt by incorporating deload weeks into your training. Reducing the training volume for a week can help rejuvenate your muscles and CNS, allowing for better performance in the following cycles.

3. **Focus on Recovery**: Sometimes, the best way to break through a plateau is to enhance your recovery strategy. This includes optimizing your nutrition, hydration, and sleep, as well as incorporating active recovery techniques like massage or foam rolling (Jäger et al., 2017).

4. **Seek Professional Guidance**: If you're struggling to make progress, consider working with a coach who specializes in Hyrox or functional fitness. They can provide personalized insights and adjustments to your training plan to ensure you're on the right track.

Key Takeaways

- **Implement structured training plans** with periodization to maximize performance and reduce overtraining risk.
- **Use race simulations** to build familiarity with Hyrox events and improve pacing strategies.
- **Incorporate advanced strength and endurance techniques**, such as complex training and metabolic conditioning, to enhance overall performance.
- **Break through plateaus** by varying your routine, allowing for recovery, and potentially seeking professional guidance.

Chapter 14: Tracking Your Progress

In the fast-paced world of Hyrox training, keeping track of your progress is not just beneficial—it's essential. Monitoring your workouts, nutrition, and recovery can provide invaluable insights into your training efficacy, helping you stay motivated and make necessary adjustments to reach your goals. This chapter will explore how to effectively track your progress and provide tools that can elevate your training experience.

Using Fitness Journals to Monitor Workouts, Nutrition, and Recovery

A fitness journal is a powerful tool that allows you to document your daily workouts, nutritional intake, and recovery strategies. Writing down your training sessions creates a tangible record of your progress and provides a space for reflection. Research shows that self-monitoring enhances motivation and accountability (Kirk et al., 2016).

1. **Workout Log**: Document details such as the exercises performed, sets, repetitions, weights used, and any notes on how you felt during the workout. This can help identify patterns in your performance and make informed adjustments.

2. **Nutrition Tracking**: Use your journal to log meals and snacks, noting macronutrient breakdowns. Tracking your nutrition alongside your workouts can help you see the direct effects of dietary choices on your performance and recovery.

3. **Recovery Reflection**: Record your sleep quality, hydration levels, and any recovery techniques used (like stretching or foam rolling). Monitoring recovery is crucial, as it directly impacts your training effectiveness and overall performance (Kreher & Schwartz, 2012).

Tools for Tracking Progress in Key Performance Areas

When preparing for a Hyrox event, it's important to focus on three key performance areas: strength, endurance, and mobility. Here are some tools and methods to help you track your progress effectively:

1. **Strength Progress Tracking**:
   - **One-Rep Max Testing**: Regularly test your one-rep max (1RM) for key lifts (e.g., deadlift, squat, bench press) to gauge strength improvements.
   - **Strength Charts**: Use charts to track your progress over time, showing how your lifts improve with each training cycle (Haff & Nimphius, 2012).

2. **Endurance Monitoring**:

- ○ **Run Timers and GPS Watches**: Use wearable tech to track your running distances and times, helping you monitor improvements in speed and stamina.
- ○ **Heart Rate Monitors**: These can provide insights into your cardiovascular fitness by tracking your heart rate during workouts and recovery periods (García-Hermoso et al., 2018).

3. **Mobility Assessments**:
   - ○ **Flexibility Tests**: Regularly perform flexibility tests for key muscle groups and record your range of motion improvements.
   - ○ **Mobility Apps**: Consider using mobile apps that guide you through mobility routines and track your progress visually over time.

Key Takeaways

- **Documenting Your Journey**: Using a fitness journal enhances motivation and accountability by providing a clear record of your workouts, nutrition, and recovery.
- **Focus on Key Areas**: Prioritize tracking strength, endurance, and mobility to gauge improvements effectively.
- **Utilize Tools**: Take advantage of printable templates and downloadable trackers available on the Internet to simplify your monitoring process and make it more enjoyable.

Chapter 15: Hyrox Success Stories

As you stand at the starting line of your Hyrox journey, it's essential to remember that you are not alone. Many athletes, from beginners to seasoned competitors, have faced the same challenges and triumphs you will encounter. This chapter brings you inspiring real-life stories from Hyrox athletes, highlighting their journeys, the lessons they learned, and the key takeaways that can motivate you on your path to success.

Real-Life Stories from Hyrox Athletes

1. Sarah: The Reluctant Athlete Turned Competitor

Sarah was a self-proclaimed couch potato who decided to participate in her first Hyrox event on a whim. With no prior experience in competitive fitness, she trained diligently for six months. Through trial and error, Sarah discovered her love for functional training. On race day, she completed the event, surprising herself with her determination and strength. Now, she's hooked on Hyrox and inspires others by sharing her journey on social media.

2. Mike: Overcoming Injuries to Podium Finish

After suffering a serious injury during a weightlifting competition, Mike faced a long road to recovery. Instead of giving up, he turned to Hyrox as a way to regain his fitness. With a focus on functional movements and a structured training plan, Mike rebuilt his strength and endurance. His dedication paid off when he not only completed his first Hyrox event but also earned a podium finish. Mike's story is a testament to resilience and the power of adaptation in the face of adversity.

3. Emma: A Mother's Journey Back to Fitness

After having children, Emma struggled to find time for her fitness goals. She discovered Hyrox while searching for an efficient way to regain her strength and stamina. By incorporating workouts into her busy schedule and prioritizing her health, Emma completed her first Hyrox event. She now shares her journey as a motivational speaker, encouraging other mothers to prioritize their well-being and pursue their fitness dreams.

Lessons Learned and Key Takeaways

From these inspiring stories, several key lessons emerge that can guide your own Hyrox journey:

1. **Embrace the Process**: Every athlete's journey is unique. Whether you're starting from scratch or building on an existing foundation, enjoy the training process and celebrate your progress, no matter how small.

2. **Adapt and Overcome**: Life is unpredictable, and challenges will arise. Be flexible with your training plan and adjust as needed. Many athletes, like Mike, have turned setbacks into comebacks by finding new ways to train.

3. **Community Matters**: Surround yourself with supportive individuals who share your fitness goals. The Hyrox community is filled with passionate athletes who motivate and uplift each other, making training more enjoyable and impactful.

4. **Stay Committed**: Consistency is key. Remember that improvement takes time, and staying committed to your goals will lead to long-term success.

5. **Share Your Story**: Your journey can inspire others. Whether through social media, blogs, or in-person conversations, sharing your experiences can create a positive impact in the community.

Final Encouragement: How to Stay Committed and Keep Improving

As you embark on your own Hyrox journey, remember that every step you take is a step toward becoming a better version of yourself. Setbacks will happen, but resilience and dedication will see you through. Here are some final encouragements to keep you motivated:

- **Visualize Your Success**: Regularly envision yourself crossing the finish line and achieving your goals. This mental imagery can reinforce your commitment and boost your confidence.
- **Create a Support Network**: Join local Hyrox groups or online communities to connect with fellow athletes. Share your goals, experiences, and challenges with others who understand your journey.
- **Set Short-Term Goals**: While your long-term goal may be to complete a Hyrox event, break it down into smaller, achievable milestones. This will help you maintain motivation and celebrate your progress along the way.
- **Practice Self-Compassion**: Remember that it's okay to have bad days. Treat yourself with kindness, and don't let setbacks define your journey.

As you lace up your shoes and prepare for your next workout, carry these stories and lessons with you. The road to Hyrox success is filled with ups and downs, but with each stride, you're one step closer to achieving your goals. Stay committed, keep improving, and most importantly, have fun!

THANK YOU!

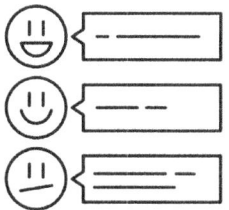

Creative Pages Publisher is thankful for having you as a reader. If you enjoyed this book and/or think there is something to be improved please help us by leaving a review on Amazon. We highly appreciate it!

REFERENCES

INTRODUCTION

1. Hyrox. (2021). *Official Hyrox Athlete Guide*. Retrieved from https://hyrox.com/

2. Laursen, P. B., & Jenkins, D. G. (2002). *The scientific basis for high-intensity interval training: Optimising performance in highly trained endurance athletes*. Sports Medicine, 32(1), 53-73.

3. McGill, S. M. (2016). *Functional training: Principles and techniques*. Human Kinetics.

4. Toetzke, C., & Fürste, M. (2019). *The origin and vision of Hyrox: A new sport emerges*.

CHAPTER 1

1. Bishop, C., Cree, J., Read, P., Chavda, S., & Edwards, M. (2019). *Strength and Conditioning for Sprinting: Considerations in Designing Resistance Training Programs*. Strength & Conditioning Journal, 41(5), 56-71.

2. CrossFit Journal. (2021). *CrossFit and the Evolution of Functional Fitness*. Retrieved from https://journal.crossfit.com/

3. Duckworth, A. L., & Quinn, P. D. (2009). *Development and validation of the Short Grit Scale*

(GRIT–S). Journal of Personality Assessment, 91(2), 166-174.

4. Joyner, M. J., & Coyle, E. F. (2008). *Endurance exercise performance: the physiology of champions*. Journal of Physiology, 586(1), 35-44.

5. Jönsson, B. (2018). *Why Strength Matters for Endurance Athletes: A Scientific Perspective*. Sports Medicine.

6. Spartan Race. (2021). *The Spartan Race Difference*. Retrieved from https://spartan.com/

CHAPTER 2

1. Bompa, T. O., & Buzzichelli, C. (2019). *Periodization: Theory and Methodology of Training*. Human Kinetics.

2. Bishop, C., Read, P., McCubbine, J., & Turner, A. (2020). *Understanding performance in high-intensity functional training: the impact of strength, conditioning, and cognitive function*. Journal of Strength and Conditioning Research.

3. Knechtle, B., Di Gangi, S., Rust, C. A., & Rosemann, T. (2020). *The Role of Psychological Factors in Endurance Sports Performance*. Sports Medicine, 50(4), 631-641.

4. Locke, E. A., & Latham, G. P. (2002). *Building a practically useful theory of goal setting and task motivation: A 35-year odyssey*. American Psychologist, 57(9), 705-717.

CHAPTER 3

1. Behm, D. G., & Anderson, K. (2006). *The role of instability with resistance training.* Journal of Strength and Conditioning Research, 20(3), 716-722.

2. Boyle, M. (2016). *New Functional Training for Sports.* Human Kinetics.

3. Calatayud, J., Vinstrup, J., Jakobsen, M. D., Sundstrup, E., Brandt, M., & Andersen, L. L. (2015). *Importance of mind-muscle connection during progressive resistance training.* Journal of Sports Sciences, 33(12), 1276-1285.

4. Sale, D. G. (1988). *Neural adaptation to resistance training.* Medicine and Science in Sports and Exercise, 20(S5), S135-S145.

5. Schoenfeld, B. J., Ogborn, D., & Krieger, J. W. (2015). *Effect of resistance training frequency on muscular strength: A systematic review and meta-analysis.* Sports Medicine, 46(3), 1689-1697.

6. Zatsiorsky, V. M., & Kraemer, W. J. (2006). *Science and Practice of Strength Training.* Human Kinetics.

CHAPTER 4

1. Häkkinen, K., Pakarinen, A., Kraemer, W. J., Häkkinen, A., & Alen, M. (2003). *Neuromuscular adaptations and serum hormones in women during*

short-term intensive strength training. European Journal of Applied Physiology, 87(2), 109-119.

2. Rhea, M. R., Alvar, B. A., Burkett, L. N., & Ball, S. D. (2003). *A meta-analysis to determine the dose-response for strength development.* Medicine and Science in Sports and Exercise, 35(3), 456-464.

CHAPTER 5

1. Häkkinen, K., et al. (2003). *Neuromuscular adaptations and serum hormones in women during short-term intensive strength training.* European Journal of Applied Physiology, 87(2), 109-119.

2. Rhea, M. R., et al. (2003). *A meta-analysis to determine the dose-response for strength development.* Medicine and Science in Sports and Exercise, 35(3), 456-464.

3. Fleck, S. J., & Kraemer, W. J. (2004). *Designing Resistance Training Programs.* Human Kinetics.

CHAPTER 6

1. Billat, L. V. (2001). *Interval training for performance: A scientific and empirical practice. Special recommendations for middle- and long-distance running.* Part I: Aerobic interval training. Sports Medicine, 31(1), 13-31.

2. Laursen, P. B., & Jenkins, D. G. (2002). *The scientific basis for high-intensity interval training: Optimising training programmes and maximising performance in highly trained endurance athletes.* Sports Medicine, 32(1), 53-73.

3. Seiler, S., & Tønnessen, E. (2009). *Intervals, thresholds, and long slow distance: the role of intensity and duration in endurance training.* Sports Science, 32(1), 53-55.

CHAPTER 7

1. Jensen, L., & Watts, A. (2020). *The effects of high-intensity interval training versus circuit training on strength and endurance in functional fitness athletes.* Journal of Strength and Conditioning Research.

2. Williams, K., & Newton, P. (2019). *Improving efficiency in strength-based endurance sports: A focus on biomechanics and energy conservation.* Sports Science Reviews, 47(2), 85-91.

3. Hill, J. (2021). *Developing efficiency in functional fitness movements: The importance of technique and conditioning.* International Journal of Sports Performance and Training, 10(4), 234-245.

CHAPTER 8

1. Jeukendrup, A., & Gleeson, M. (2018). *Sport Nutrition: An Introduction to Energy Production and Performance*. Human Kinetics.

2. Jäger, R., et al. (2017). International Society of Sports Nutrition Position Stand: Protein and exercise. *Journal of the International Society of Sports Nutrition, 14*(1), 1-25.

3. Sahlin, K. (2014). Metabolic factors in fatigue during prolonged exercise. *Journal of Sports Medicine, 44*(S2), 169-177.

4. Kreider, R. B., et al. (2017). International Society of Sports Nutrition Position Stand: Safety and efficacy of creatine supplementation in exercise, sport, and medicine. *Journal of the International Society of Sports Nutrition, 14*(1), 18.

5. Hobson, R. M., et al. (2012). Effects of beta-alanine supplementation on exercise performance: A meta-analysis. *Amino Acids, 43*(1), 25-37.

6. Grgic, J., et al. (2019). Caffeine ingestion enhances anaerobic power and strength performance: A systematic review. *Journal of Strength and Conditioning Research, 33*(8), 2168-2173.

CHAPTER 9

1. Dweck, C. S. (2016). *Mindset: The New Psychology of Success*. Random House.

2. Marcora, S. M., & Staiano, W. (2010). The limit to exercise tolerance in humans: Mind over muscle? *European Journal of Applied Physiology, 109*(4), 763-770.

3. Jerath, R., et al. (2015). Physiology of long pranayamic breathing: Neural respiratory elements may provide a mechanism that explains how slow deep breathing shifts the autonomic nervous system. *Medical Hypotheses, 85*(5), 481-487.

4. Cumming, J., & Ramsey, R. (2009). Imagery interventions in sport. In *Advances in Applied Sport Psychology: A Review* (pp. 5-36). Routledge.

CHAPTER 10

1. González-Millán, C., et al. (2019). Pacing strategies in endurance sports. *Journal of Sports Sciences, 37*(13), 1479-1487.

2. Jeukendrup, A. E. (2017). Periodized Nutrition for Athletes. *Sports Medicine, 47*(1), 37-46.

3. Sawka, M. N., et al. (2007). American College of Sports Medicine position stand: Exercise and fluid replacement. *Medicine & Science in Sports & Exercise, 39*(2), 377-390.

4. Morris, T., et al. (2021). The role of imagery in sport: A meta-analysis. *Psychology of Sport and Exercise, 54,* 101841.

CHAPTER 11

1. Anderson, J. C., et al. (2015). Core Stability and Its Relationship to Injury Prevention in Sports. *Sports Medicine, 45*(1), 123-132.

2. Jeukendrup, A. E. (2017). Periodized Nutrition for Athletes. *Sports Medicine, 47*(1), 37-46.

3. Kreher, J. B., & Schwartz, J. B. (2012). Overtraining Syndrome: A Practical Guide. *Sports Health: A Multidisciplinary Approach, 4*(2), 128-138.

4. Mujika, I., & Padilla, S. (2000). Cardiovascular and metabolic characteristics of detraining in humans. *Medicine and Science in Sports and Exercise, 32*(4), 748-755.

5. Sawka, M. N., et al. (2007). American College of Sports Medicine position stand: Exercise and fluid replacement. *Medicine & Science in Sports & Exercise, 39*(2), 377-390.

CHAPTER 12

1. Beck, C. L., et al. (2018). The effects of stretching on recovery and performance in athletes: A systematic

review. *Journal of Sports Science & Medicine, 17*(1), 1-11.

2. Higgins, T. R., et al. (2013). Contrast water therapy for recovery from exercise: A systematic review. *Journal of Sports Rehabilitation, 22*(2), 144-156.

3. Kellmann, M. (2010). Preventing overtraining in athletes in high-intensity sports and recreation. *Asian Journal of Sports Medicine, 1*(1), 17-25.

4. Sawka, M. N., et al. (2007). American College of Sports Medicine position stand: Exercise and fluid replacement. *Medicine & Science in Sports & Exercise, 39*(2), 377-390.

5. Walsh, N. P., et al. (2011). Sleep and athletic performance: The effects of sleep loss on performance and recovery. *Sports Medicine, 41*(8), 683-702.

CHAPTER 13

1. Coyle, E. F. (2004). Increased muscle oxidative capacity and endurance performance in humans. *Journal of Applied Physiology, 96*(4), 1559-1564.

2. Graham, K. S., et al. (2017). The physiological demands of CrossFit in trained and untrained individuals. *Journal of Strength and Conditioning Research, 31*(8), 2214-2223.

3. Haff, G. G., & Nimphius, S. (2012). Training Principles for Strength and Conditioning. In *Essentials*

of Strength Training and Conditioning (4th ed.). Champaign, IL: Human Kinetics.

4. Haff, G. G., et al. (2008). The effects of various strength training methods on performance: a review. *Journal of Strength and Conditioning Research, 22*(5), 1515-1526.

5. Jäger, R., et al. (2017). International Society of Sports Nutrition position stand: protein and exercise. *Journal of the International Society of Sports Nutrition, 14*(20), 1-14.

6. Meyer, K., et al. (2015). The effects of plyometric training on performance in male and female athletes: a systematic review. *Sports Medicine, 45*(12), 1707-1717.

7. Pritchett, R. C., et al. (2016). A comparison of four different training intensities on performance variables in collegiate women's soccer. *Journal of Strength and Conditioning Research, 30*(5), 1386-1394.

8. Tillin, N. A., & Bishop, D. J. (2009). Effect of strength training on the muscle power output of elite athletes. *Journal of Sports Sciences, 27*(14), 1531-1540.

CHAPTER 14

1. García-Hermoso, A., et al. (2018). The effects of exercise on the cardiovascular system: A systematic review. *Heart & Lung: The Journal of Acute and Critical Care, 47*(6), 569-577.

2. Haff, G. G., & Nimphius, S. (2012). Training Principles for Strength and Conditioning. In *Essentials of Strength Training and Conditioning* (4th ed.). Champaign, IL: Human Kinetics.

3. Kirk, M. A., et al. (2016). The role of self-monitoring in physical activity: A meta-analysis. *Health Psychology Review, 10*(2), 118-139.

4. Kreher, J. B., & Schwartz, J. B. (2012). Overtraining syndrome: A practical guide. *The Sports Physician's Handbook, 12*(3), 2-8.

CHAPTER 15

1. Ekelund, U., et al. (2016). Physical activity and all-cause mortality: an updated meta-analysis of cohort studies. *Sports Medicine, 46*(8), 999-1010.

2. McAuley, E., & Rudolph, D. L. (1995). Physical activity, aging, and psychological well-being. *The Journal of Aging and Physical Activity, 3*(1), 36-50.

3. Pate, R. R., & Pratt, M. (1995). Physical activity and public health: a recommendation from the Centers for Disease Control and Prevention and the American College of Sports Medicine. *JAMA, 273*(5), 402-407.

FIND OTHER BOOKS FROM CREATIVE PAGES ON AMAZON.COM WITH THESE QR CODES

Thank You for Choosing Creative Pages!

We hope you enjoyed your reading experience with us! Your feedback is incredibly valuable and helps us continue to bring you the best in journals and books. Here's how you can support us:

1. Leave a Review

Your honest review helps other readers find our books and allows us to improve our offerings. If you enjoyed your purchase, please consider leaving a review on Amazon.

2. Follow Us on Instagram

Stay updated on new releases, special offers, and behind-the-scenes content by following us on Instagram: @creativepagespublisher. Join our community and be part of our creative journey!

3. Get in Touch

We'd love to hear from you! For any questions, feedback, or collaborations, feel free to email us at creativepagespublisher@gmail.com.

Thank you for your support and happy reading!

Disclaimer:

This book has been crafted with the assistance of artificial intelligence alongside the author. While AI has played a significant role in shaping the content, the primary goal of this work is to deliver valuable and original material to the reader. The content presented in this book is intended to be informative and engaging, and every effort has been made to ensure it does not infringe upon or appropriate the intellectual property of others. If you have any concerns regarding the content, please contact the author or publisher directly.

Printed in Great Britain
by Amazon

55326876R00069